The Boxers
(9,059 words)

MARY TOMALIN

Level 3

Series Editors: Andy Hopkins and Jocelyn Potter

Pearson Education Limited
Edinburgh Gate, Harlow,
Essex CM20 2JE, England
and Associated Companies throughout the world.

ISBN 0 997 80580 3

First published by Penguin Books 2003
This edition published 2006

1 3 5 7 9 10 8 6 4 2

Text copyright © Mary Tomalin 2003
Illustrations copyright © Philip Bannister (Illustration) 2003

The moral rights of the author and illustrator have been asserted.

All rights reserved

Typeset by Pantek Arts Ltd, Maidstone, Kent
Set in 11/14pt Bembo
Printed in China
SWTC/01

All rights reserved; no part of this publication may be reproduced, stored in a retrieval system, or transmitted in any form or by any means, electronic, mechanical, photocopying, recording or otherwise, without the prior written permission of the Publishers.

Published by Pearson Education Limited in association with
Penguin Books Ltd, both companies being subsidiaries of Pearson Plc

---

For a complete list of the titles available in the Penguin Readers series please write to your local Pearson Education office or to: Penguin Readers Marketing Department, Pearson Education, Edinburgh Gate, Harlow, Essex, CM20 2JE.

Contents

	page
Introduction	iv
The People in the Play	viii
Act 1 Monday Morning	1
Act 2 Monday Afternoon	11
Act 3 Tuesday Morning	23
Act 4 Tuesday Afternoon	30
Activities	38

Introduction

PROSECUTION: *Mrs Radman, why did you lie to the police about the bruise on your face?*
JENNIFER RADMAN: *I was frightened.*
PROSECUTION: *You were right to be frightened, Mrs Radman. You are a murderer.*

When Michael Boxer's cleaner goes into his sitting room one morning, she finds his dead body. Someone has hit him on the head and killed him. But where is the murder weapon? And who is the murderer?

The Boxers are not always a happy family. The police think that Michael's sister, Jennifer Radman, killed her brother. Jennifer was at Michael's house on the night of the murder. She needed money, and he refused to give it to her. But did she kill him?

Michael Boxer was a policeman. There were other people who hated him too. But how much did they hate him? As much as his sister? What do you think? Read the play and decide.

Mary Tomalin writes books for teaching and learning English, and she has written other Penguin Readers. She also helps British people with their personal problems. She likes the fact that the two jobs are so different. Mary lives in the south of England and is married with one son.

Reading and acting the play

You can read *The Boxers* silently, like any story in a book, imagining the court, the people, their clothes and their voices from the words on the page and the pictures. You can also listen to the cassette as you read. Or you can read the story first, then listen to the cassette later.

But *The Boxers* is a play, so a group of people can speak the words. This is very different from silent reading, because you bring the people in the play to life. They can sound interested, sad or angry. You can add silence and the noises of people in a courtroom. The group can also stop and discuss the play. What does this person mean? Why does he or she say that?

You can have more fun if you act the play. Place chairs and tables carefully to make a courtroom. The picture on pages vi and vii will help you. People always stand up when they speak in a courtroom. The judge always sits. Everybody watches the judge, the lawyers and the witnesses as they speak. They also watch the jury. Spectators sometimes make noises when they are excited. Hands and faces show people's feelings. As you practise the play, you can act the same scene more than once. It will get better and better.

At the end of the play, the jury must discuss the charge against Jennifer Radman and decide. Did she kill her brother? Give your reasons. You must be sure.

This is an imaginary story. The people in it act and speak in a similar way to people in real English courts, but there are differences. These make the play more interesting.

There are other Penguin Readers plays. If you act this play in front of another group, perhaps they will act a different play for your group. You can read *The Boxers* or you can act the play, but have fun and enjoy it!

THE COURT

Member of the jury

Jury

Prosecution lawyer

Defence lawyer

Spectators

The People in the Play

JUDGE (called 'your Honour' in court)
MRS COLLY, the clerk of the court
JENNIFER RADMAN, 35, the defendant, short and thin
MR FROST, 45, the prosecution lawyer
MR GILES, 34, the defence lawyer
TWELVE MEMBERS OF THE JURY
SPECTATORS

Witnesses for the Prosecution
GINA LOPEZ, 28, a waitress in a Spanish restaurant
PETER LAMPTON, 71, a friend of Jennifer Radman's father
TIM RADLEY, 35, Jennifer Radman's bank manager
ROBERT WOODS, 45, the owner of Jennifer Radman's flat
MATTHEW FOLEY, 35, a neighbour of Michael Boxer
PAMELA STANTON, 52, Michael Boxer's cleaner
HARRY ROSS, 36, a forensic officer
WILLIAM BROWN, 47, a police detective
SIMON NICHOLS, 63, a neighbour of Jennifer Radman

Witnesses for the Defence
ALICE O'CONNELL, 44, a head teacher
SARAH ROSE, 25, a neighbour of Jennifer Radman
JONATHAN PETERS, 66, a friend of Michael Boxer
DANIEL RADMAN, 18, Jennifer Radman's eldest son
SHARON PHILLIPS, 18, Daniel Radman's girlfriend

Act 1 Monday Morning

Scene 1

[*The courtroom is in an old building in the south of England. It is a November morning. In the courtroom are the defendant, the defence lawyer, the prosecution lawyer, the clerk and the twelve members of the jury. There are about thirty spectators. The defendant looks nervous. The jury members look excited. Everyone stands as the judge walks in. He sits down and puts on his glasses.*]

JUDGE [*looking round*]: Please sit down. [*Everyone sits.*] Let's begin. Please read the charge, Mrs Colly.

[*The clerk stands up.*]

CLERK: The defendant is Mrs Jennifer Radman, aged thirty-five. Mrs Radman is charged with murdering her brother, Michael Boxer, on the night of December 14th last year.

JUDGE: Mr Frost, please begin.

[*The prosecution lawyer stands.*]

PROSECUTION LAWYER [*speaking in a loud voice*]: Your Honour, members of the jury, Jennifer Radman's father, David Boxer, was a rich man. Her brother, Michael Boxer, was ten years older than her. The defendant left home at the age of sixteen. She went to live with her boyfriend and had two children by him. Mrs Radman's boyfriend left her when she was nineteen. She didn't go out to work. After her boyfriend left, she had a number of different boyfriends. When the defendant was twenty-eight, she married. She had two more children, now four and five years old. The defendant's husband left her two years ago, and she lives alone with her four children. Mrs Radman saw her father about once every two years. They always quarrelled. The defendant also quarrelled with her brother when she saw him.

DEFENCE LAWYER [*standing*]: Your Honour, the prosecution must *prove* that they quarrelled. [*He sits down.*]

JUDGE: Yes. Mr Frost, you must prove that.

PROSECUTION: Yes, your Honour. [*turning to the jury*] Members of the jury, you will hear that the defendant saw her father, David Boxer, on November 23rd last year. She asked him for money, but he refused. A week later, he died of heart problems. Witnesses saw the defendant quarrel with her brother at their father's funeral. Again, she asked for money and was refused. You will hear that on the night of December 14th, the defendant visited her brother. That night, Michael Boxer was murdered. Someone hit him on the back of the head and killed him. We believe that the murderer was Jennifer Radman. [*He sits down.*]

JUDGE: Mr Giles . . .

DEFENCE [*walking up to the jury*]: Members of the jury, we do not believe that Jennifer Radman killed her brother. It is true that Mrs Radman needed money. But she is a good mother and a good woman. She is not violent. We have witnesses who will say this. Mrs Radman went to her brother's house on the night of December 14th. But that does not mean she killed him. And he left her no money in his will. Michael Radman was a policeman and a lot of people hated him. We believe that one of these people killed him. We believe we can prove this. [*He sits down.*]

Scene 2

CLERK: Call the first witness for the prosecution – Mrs Gina Lopez.

[*Gina Lopez comes into the court and goes to the witness box.*]

PROSECUTION [*standing*]: Mrs Lopez, what is your job?

GINA LOPEZ [*speaking quietly*]: I'm a waitress. I work at La Rueda, a Spanish restaurant in north London.

PROSECUTION: And what happened on the evening of November 23rd?

GINA LOPEZ: A man of about seventy-five and a woman in her early thirties came into the restaurant.

PROSECUTION [*pointing to the defendant*]: Is that the woman?

GINA LOPEZ [*looking carefully at the defendant*]: Yes.

PROSECUTION [*holding up a photograph of David Boxer*] And is this the man? This is photograph one, members of the jury, a photograph of the defendant's father, David Boxer.

GINA LOPEZ [*looking carefully at the photo*]: Yes. [*The clerk shows the photo to the members of the jury.*] The man and the woman quarrelled all through the meal. I remember the woman saying, 'I really need the money, Dad. Please help me.' They both got very angry. I heard the man say, 'I'm leaving all my money to your brother. You're not going to get anything from me.'

PROSECUTION: How did the defendant look when her father said that?

GINA LOPEZ: Very upset and angry.

PROSECUTION [*interested*]: What happened next?

GINA LOPEZ: The woman stood up and walked out of the restaurant.

PROSECUTION: Did she say anything to you or to Mr Boxer?

GINA LOPEZ [*speaking excitedly*]: She said to the man, 'Goodbye, you pig. This is the last time you'll see me.'

PROSECUTION [*smiling*]: Thank you. I have no more questions. Your witness, Mr Giles. [*He sits down.*]

DEFENCE [*walking up to Mrs Lopez*]: You say the defendant was very angry. How did she show that?

GINA LOPEZ: She just *looked* angry. And the sound of her voice made it clear too.

DEFENCE: She didn't shout at him?
GINA LOPEZ [*after a minute*]: No, she didn't.
DEFENCE: How did David Boxer show he was angry?
GINA LOPEZ: He shouted a lot. And he was rude to me.
DEFENCE: What did he say?
GINA LOPEZ: He said something like, 'Hurry up! We haven't got all day!' I was really angry.
DEFENCE [*politely*]: Thank you. I have no more questions. [*He sits down.*]
JUDGE: Mr Frost?
PROSECUTION: No more questions, your Honour.

Scene 3

CLERK: Call Mr Peter Lampton.

[*Peter Lampton comes into the court and goes to the witness box. He walks with difficulty.*]

PROSECUTION: Do you work, Mr Lampton?
PETER LAMPTON [*speaking in a deep voice*]: No, not now – I'm seventy-one. I was a lawyer.
PROSECUTION: Mr Lampton, you were a friend of David Boxer?
PETER LAMPTON: Yes, we were at school together.
PROSECUTION: David Boxer died on December 1st. Can you describe what happened between Mrs Radman and her brother on the day of David Boxer's funeral, on December 8th?
PETER LAMPTON: Yes. It was almost the end of the funeral. I was standing next to Michael and Jennifer and they were quarrelling quite loudly. I heard Jennifer say, 'Michael, I've got big debts. I need £4,000. You're getting all Dad's money. Surely you can give me two or three thousand?'
PROSECUTION: And what did Michael Boxer reply?
PETER LAMPTON: He said, 'I earned that money. I saw Dad every two weeks. What did you ever do for him?'

PROSECUTION: And what did the defendant reply?

PETER LAMPTON: She didn't. It was true. She didn't often see her father.

PROSECUTION: Did you hear any more of the conversation between Jennifer and her brother?

PETER LAMPTON [*angrily*]: Yes! Just before Jennifer walked away, she said, 'You should be dead too!' I thought, 'That's Jennifer!'

PROSECUTION: What did David Boxer tell you about his daughter, Mr Lampton?

PETER LAMPTON: Oh, he told me a lot. And I knew her when she was young, of course. She was always in trouble at school, she had a baby at sixteen ... she didn't work ... When Jennifer saw her father, she always asked him for money. She was always in debt.

PROSECUTION: Thank you. I have no more questions. Your witness, Mr Giles. [*He sits down.*]

DEFENCE [*walking up to Peter Lampton*]: Those words of the defendant: 'You should be dead too!' ... What did you understand from them, Mr Lampton?

PETER LAMPTON [*after thinking for a minute*]: She was angry. I think that she really hated Michael then.

DEFENCE: How much did she hate him? Enough to kill him? What did you think at the time?

PETER LAMPTON [*surprised*]: No, no. She was just angry.

DEFENCE: Thank you. Mr Lampton, was Jennifer Radman's life easy when she was a child?

PETER LAMPTON: No – no, life wasn't easy for her.

DEFENCE: Can you explain why not?

PETER LAMPTON [*looking uncomfortable*]: I can't say that David Boxer was a very good father. His wife died when Jennifer was two. David was always busy. He – he didn't have much time for Jennifer.

DEFENCE: Mr Lampton, Jennifer left home at sixteen. Can you understand why?

'You should be dead too!'

Peter Lampton: Yes, of course. She was very unhappy. But she was too young to have a child. That was stupid! And her boyfriend was a criminal, you know!

Defence [*trying to hide his surprise*]: What do you mean by that, Mr Lampton?

Peter Lampton: He stole a car. And he was caught.

Defence [*coldly*]: The defendant and her boyfriend were very young. Thank you, Mr Lampton. I have no more questions. [*He sits down.*]

Scene 4

Clerk: Call Mr Tim Radley.

[*Tim Radley walks quickly into the court and goes to the witness box.*]

Prosecution [*standing and speaking in a friendly way*]: Mr Radley, what is your job?

Tim Radley [*looking very serious*]: I'm a bank manager.

Prosecution: Can you describe the defendant's visit to your bank on December 11th last year?

Tim Radley: Yes. Mrs Radman wanted the bank to lend her £5,000. She had debts of £4,000. She couldn't pay the rent on her flat, and she didn't want to lose it.

Prosecution: Did you lend the defendant the money?

Tim Radley [*looking at the floor*]: No, I didn't. I didn't feel it was a good idea.

Prosecution: How did the defendant seem?

Tim Radley: She was very upset when I said no. She didn't want to leave. I had to ask her to go.

Prosecution: That's all. Your witness, Mr Giles. [*He sits down.*]

Defence [*standing*]: What did Mrs Radman tell you about her plans for the future, Mr Radley?

TIM RADLEY [*thinking for a minute*]: Ah. Yes. She did tell me about her plans. She was working in a shop for three or four hours a day. She planned to get a nine-to-five job when her youngest child started school. She said, 'When I do that, I can easily pay the money back.'

DEFENCE: So Mrs Radman hoped to pay her debts?

TIM RADLEY: Yes, she did.

DEFENCE: I have no more questions. [*He sits down.*]

Scene 5

CLERK: Call Mr Robert Woods.

[*Robert Woods comes into the court and goes to the witness box.*]

PROSECUTION [*standing*]: What do you do, Mr Woods?

ROBERT WOODS [*speaking fast*]: I own a number of flats. Mrs Radman lives in one of them.

PROSECUTION: Does Mrs Radman always pay her rent on time?

ROBERT WOODS: No. Last year she didn't pay anything for six months. I went to see her in early December. I wanted the money – or the flat. I was ready to go to court.

PROSECUTION: And what did the defendant reply?

ROBERT WOODS [*looking worried*]: She started to cry. She said, 'Oh no, not court. I'll lose everything.'

PROSECUTION [*smiling*]: Thank you. Your witness, Mr Giles. [*He sits down.*]

DEFENCE [*standing*]: Mr Woods, did you ask Mrs Radman about her plans to pay you back?

ROBERT WOODS: No, I didn't. I don't think she had any.

DEFENCE: How can you be sure of that?

ROBERT WOODS [*thinking for a minute*]: I can't be sure. I didn't ask.

DEFENCE: Thank you. I have no more questions. [*He sits down.*]

Scene 6

CLERK: Call Mr Matthew Foley.

[*Matthew Foley comes into the court and walks quickly to the witness box. He looks nervous.*]

PROSECUTION [*standing*]: Can you explain how you knew Michael Boxer, Mr Foley?

MATTHEW FOLEY [*speaking slowly*]: I live next door to him. I didn't know him well, but I often saw him, of course.

PROSECUTION: Can you tell the jury what you saw on the night of December 14th?

MATTHEW FOLEY: Yes. I looked out of the window at about 8.30 p.m. and saw a blue Volkswagen.

PROSECUTION: Whose car was that? Do you know?

MATTHEW FOLEY: That's Mrs Radman's car. I've seen her get out of it before.

PROSECUTION: And how long was the car outside Mr Boxer's house?

MATTHEW FOLEY [*thinking for a minute*]: I can't be sure. I took the dog out for a walk at 9.00. Her car was still there when I returned at 9.30.

PROSECUTION: Was it there later?

MATTHEW FOLEY [*looking worried*]: I don't know. I went inside and didn't look out again. So I can't say.

PROSECUTION: But you're sure the car was there at 9.30?

MATTHEW FOLEY: Yes, I'm sure of that.

PROSECUTION: That's all, Mr Foley. Your witness, Mr Giles. [*He sits down.*]

DEFENCE [*standing*]: Mr Foley, you say that you didn't look outside again after 9.30.

MATTHEW FOLEY: That's correct.

DEFENCE: So it's possible that Mrs Radman left her brother's house at 9.35 or 9.40?

MATTHEW FOLEY: Yes, it's possible. I was watching television.

DEFENCE [*walking to the jury*]: Thank you, Mr Foley. I have no more questions. [*He sits down.*]

JUDGE [*taking off his glasses*]: The court will stop for lunch and return at 2 o'clock.

Act 2 Monday Afternoon

Scene 1

[*The judge comes into the court and everyone stands. He sits down.*]

JUDGE: Please sit down. [*Everyone sits. He speaks to the clerk.*] Please begin.
CLERK: Call Mrs Pamela Stanton.

[*Pamela Stanton comes into the courtroom. She walks to the witness box with her head down. She looks unhappy.*]

PROSECUTION [*standing and smiling warmly*]: Mrs Stanton, how did you know Michael Boxer?
PAMELA STANTON [*speaking quietly*]: I was his cleaner. I cleaned his house for fifteen years.
PROSECUTION: And what happened on the morning of December 15th?
PAMELA STANTON: I went to his house to clean twice a week. I have my own key, so I opened the door. It was 10 o'clock. Mr Boxer was at work – I thought. I got the cleaning things from the cupboard under the stairs, and cleaned downstairs. Then I went up to the sitting room.
PROSECUTION: What time was that, Mrs Stanton?
PAMELA STANTON: It was probably about 11 o'clock.
PROSECUTION: Please continue.
PAMELA STANTON: I went upstairs. [*Her voice starts to shake.*] I went into the sitting room – and there he was. On the floor. There was a lot of blood. [*She starts to cry.*]
PROSECUTION [*speaking kindly*]: I'm sorry, but I have to ask you more questions, Mrs Stanton.
JUDGE: Please give Mrs Stanton a chair.

[*The clerk brings Mrs Stanton a chair and she sits down.*]

'I went into the sitting room – and there he was.'

PAMELA STANTON: I'm all right now.
PROSECUTION: Can you describe the body, Mrs Stanton?
PAMELA STANTON [*slowly*]: He was lying on his front, about three metres from the sitting-room door. The back of his head was all bloody. [*She cries again.*]
JUDGE: Please give Mrs Stanton a few minutes.
PROSECUTION: Yes, your Honour . . . [*He waits until Mrs Stanton stops crying.*] What did you do next?
PAMELA STANTON [*looking up and drying her eyes*]: I called the police. And then I looked round the room. I noticed something. Mr Boxer kept a big stone sculpture on a shelf along the wall – and it was gone.
PROSECUTION: Can you describe the sculpture, Mrs Stanton?
PAMELA STANTON: It was a grey stone sculpture of a man's head. It was very big and heavy, but it wasn't expensive. I know because Mr Boxer told me. A friend gave it to him a long time ago. It was from somewhere in Asia.
PROSECUTION: Thank you, Mrs Stanton. Mrs Colly, can you show Mrs Stanton the pieces of stone, please? [*The clerk puts a plastic bag on the table near to the witness box. In it are some very small pieces of stone.*] Mrs Stanton, can you look at these very carefully? Have you seen stone like this before?

[*Mrs Stanton leaves the witness box and goes to the table. She picks up the bag and looks carefully at the pieces of stone.*]

PAMELA STANTON: Yes, they're the same colour and the same kind of stone as the sculpture.
PROSECUTION: Thank you. Members of the jury, we'll learn more about these pieces of stone from the next witness. [*turning back to Pamela Stanton*] Mrs Stanton, what did you do while you waited for the police?
PAMELA STANTON: I ran around the house, looking at the windows. They were all closed and locked. And everything was there. Only the sculpture was missing.

PROSECUTION [*to the jury*]: That's interesting. So the killer was not an ordinary thief. [*turning back to Mrs Stanton*] I'd like to ask you another question, Mrs Stanton. Did any other person have a key to Mr Boxer's house?

PAMELA STANTON: No, there were only two keys. Mr Boxer had one and I had the other. And he changed all the locks a week before he was killed.

PROSECUTION: Why did he do that, Mrs Stanton. Do you know?

PAMELA STANTON: No, I don't. He didn't tell me.

PROSECUTION: Thank you. One more question, Mrs Stanton. Where were you on the night of the murder?

PAMELA STANTON [*looking very upset*]: I was out with three friends. We went to the cinema.

PROSECUTION [*smiling*]: Thank you, Mrs Stanton. Your witness, Mr Giles. [*He sits down.*]

Scene 2

DEFENCE [*standing and looking very serious*]: Now, Mrs Stanton, I want you to think carefully about this question. The stone sculpture ... were you able to lift it easily?

PAMELA STANTON: No, it was difficult to lift. It was very heavy.

DEFENCE: How often did you lift it?

PAMELA STANTON: Never. I cleaned round it.

DEFENCE: Thank you, Mrs Stanton. Now, could you look carefully at Mrs Radman, please? [*Mrs Stanton looks at Jennifer Radman.*] Is Mrs Radman heavier or lighter than you, do you think?

PAMELA STANTON: She's lighter than me. She's shorter and thinner.

DEFENCE [*speaking slowly*]: Now, I want you to think very carefully before you answer these questions. Is Mrs Radman strong enough to lift that stone sculpture? Could she kill her brother with it?

PROSECUTION [*standing*]: Your Honour, Mrs Stanton can only *guess* the answer to those questions. [*He sits down.*]

JUDGE: Yes – Mrs Stanton, please do not answer.

DEFENCE: Mrs Stanton, I'm going to repeat your words. The sculpture was 'difficult to lift'. You never lifted it. Is that correct?

PAMELA STANTON: Yes, it is.

DEFENCE [*smiling*]: Thank you, Mrs Stanton. [*turning to the jury*] Members of the jury, do you understand what that means? The stone sculpture was not there the morning after the murder. We know that someone hit Michael Boxer on the back of the head with something very heavy. So the sculpture was probably the murder weapon. But Mrs Stanton says that she could not lift the sculpture.

PROSECUTION [*standing*]: Your Honour, Mrs Stanton did *not* say that. She said, 'It was difficult to lift.' [*He sits down.*]

JUDGE: That is correct.

DEFENCE: Members of the jury, please look carefully at Jennifer Radman. As Mrs Stanton says, the defendant is shorter and thinner than her. How could Jennifer Radman lift the sculpture – lift it and kill someone with it? She isn't strong enough. Doesn't this show that Mrs Radman was *not* her brother's killer? [*He looks silently at the jury.*]

JUDGE [*coughing*]: Please continue, Mr Giles.

DEFENCE: Mrs Stanton, were there signs of a fight in the sitting room? For example, was furniture in the wrong position?

PAMELA STANTON: No, everything was in its place – except the sculpture.

DEFENCE [*walking closer*]: Are you sure about that?

PAMELA STANTON: I am.

DEFENCE: Members of the jury, Michael Boxer was killed, but there were no signs of a fight. If Mrs Radman and her brother quarrelled that night, they did not fight violently or for long.

[*He is silent for a minute.*] One last question, Mrs Stanton. In your opinion, did Mrs Radman kill her brother?

JUDGE [*speaking angrily*]: Mr Giles, you know you cannot ask that question.

DEFENCE: I'm sorry, your Honour. Thank you, Mrs Stanton. You can go now. [*He sits down.*]

Scene 3

CLERK: Call Mr Harry Ross.

[*Harry Ross comes into the court and goes to the witness box.*]

PROSECUTION [*standing*]: Mr Ross, can you describe your job?

HARRY ROSS [*speaking in a loud voice*]: Yes, I'm a forensic officer. I was asked to look at Michael Boxer's body after his death.

PROSECUTION: Thank you. Can you tell the members of the jury how Mr Boxer died?

HARRY ROSS: Michael Boxer was hit on the back of the head with something very heavy. That killed him.

PROSECUTION: So his death wasn't an accident? He didn't fall?

HARRY ROSS: No.

PROSECUTION: Mrs Colly, could you pass photographs two to eight to the jury? These show Mr Boxer's body.

[*The clerk gives the photographs to the jury. Each member of the jury looks at them carefully.*]

PROSECUTION: What was the time of death?

HARRY ROSS [*speaking carefully*]: In my opinion, he was killed sometime between 10 o'clock and 11.30 on the night of December 14th.

PROSECUTION: Members of the jury, please remember this. Between 10 o'clock and 11.30. We know that Jennifer Radman's car was outside her brother's house at 9.30. Mr Ross, what did you discover when you looked at the body?

HARRY ROSS: I found very small pieces of grey stone in the back of the dead man's head.

PROSECUTION: And where do you think these pieces of stone came from?

HARRY ROSS: We found similar pieces on the shelf in the sitting room. We asked Mrs Stanton to look at them. She was sure that they were from a stone sculpture from somewhere in Asia. The sculpture wasn't there, so I haven't seen it. But our tests show that the stone probably came from the Philippines.

PROSECUTION [*turning to the jury*]: Members of the jury, Mr Ross believes that the sculpture was the murder weapon. The prosecution believes that Jennifer Radman killed her brother with the sculpture. When someone is very angry, they are very strong. Boxer had his back to his sister. She lifted the sculpture and hit him on the back of the head. Is this possible, in your opinion, Mr Ross?

HARRY ROSS: Yes, it's possible.

DEFENCE [*standing*]: Your Honour, how can Mr Ross know that the defendant was able to lift the sculpture? He has not even seen it.

JUDGE: I agree, Mr Giles. Members of the jury, Mr Ross cannot know that.

PROSECUTION: Can you continue with your description of your examination of the body, Mr Ross?

HARRY ROSS: Yes. There were long scratches on Michael Boxer's face and around his neck.

PROSECUTION: Mrs Colly, please pass photographs nine and ten, photographs of the face and neck, to the jury. [*The clerk passes the photos to the jury. They look at them carefully. Mr Frost turns back to Mr Ross.*] Was there blood in the scratches?

HARRY ROSS: No, no blood.

PROSECUTION: And what did you find when you did an examination of Mrs Radman later?

HARRY ROSS: There were small pieces of Michael Boxer's skin under Mrs Radman's fingernails.

PROSECUTION: What does this tell us, Mr Ross?

HARRY ROSS: It tells us that Mrs Radman scratched her brother.

PROSECUTION: Thank you. [*He thinks for a minute.*] Is that all you found?

HARRY ROSS: No. I also found some stone dust on Mrs Radman's clothes. It was the same stone as the pieces in Mr Boxer's head.

PROSECUTION [*smiling*]: Thank you. I have no more questions. [*He sits down.*]

DEFENCE [*standing*]: Mr Ross, did you look at Mrs Radman's face?

HARRY ROSS: I did.

DEFENCE: Can you tell us what you found?

HARRY ROSS: Yes. There was a large bruise on the left side of her face.

DEFENCE: What do you think this means?

HARRY ROSS [*looking bored*]: Perhaps Michael Boxer hit her. Perhaps she did it herself. I have no idea.

DEFENCE [*coldly*]: You found stone dust from the sculpture on Jennifer Radman's clothes. Perhaps she touched the sculpture while she walked round the room. Perhaps she then touched her clothes. Is that possible, do you think?

HARRY ROSS [*not wanting to agree*]: Yes.

DEFENCE: Thank you, Mr Ross. I have no more questions. [*He sits down.*]

Scene 4

CLERK: Call police detective William Brown.

[*Police detective William Brown comes into the court. He walks to the witness box.*]

PROSECUTION [*standing*]: What is your job, Detective Brown?

WILLIAM BROWN [*speaking clearly*]: I'm a police detective. I was the detective who went to Michael Boxer's home after the murder.

PROSECUTION: Can you tell the court what you did? Can you also say what you found?

WILLIAM BROWN: We looked at all the doors and windows. No locks were broken and the doors and windows were all locked. All of them.

PROSECUTION: So how did the killer get into the house, do you think?

WILLIAM BROWN: Michael Boxer probably opened the door. He probably knew his killer.

PROSECUTION [*to the jury*]: Perhaps that person was a member of his own family, members of the jury. [*turning back to Detective Brown*] Detective Brown, were there signs of a fight near the front door?

WILLIAM BROWN [*very sure*]: No, none.

PROSECUTION: Thank you. But there's another possibility. Perhaps Michael Boxer opened the door to someone who was carrying a gun or a knife?

WILLIAM BROWN: Yes, that's possible.

PROSECUTION: But then why didn't this person use the weapon to kill Michael Boxer?

WILLIAM BROWN: That's a good question. I don't know.

PROSECUTION: So Boxer probably knew his murderer. Do you agree?

WILLIAM BROWN [*looking at Jennifer Radman*]: That's my opinion – yes.

PROSECUTION [*looking very serious*]: Thank you, Detective Brown. I have no more questions. Your witness, Mr Giles. [*He sits down.*]

DEFENCE [*standing*]: Detective Brown, isn't it possible that Michael Boxer opened his door to someone with a knife or a gun... They followed him to the sitting room. They told him to turn round. They picked up the sculpture and killed him with it. That was a very clever thing to do. As a result, the police believe that Michael opened the door to a friend or to someone in his family.

WILLIAM BROWN [*slowly*]: Yes, it is possible. A lot of things are *possible*. But I don't think it happened. People with guns and knives use them, you know.

DEFENCE: Not always, Detective Brown. [*He is silent for a minute.*] Have you found the sculpture?

WILLIAM BROWN: No, we haven't.

DEFENCE: Did you search Mrs Radman's house and garden? And her car?

WILLIAM BROWN: We did. We didn't find the weapon.

DEFENCE [*turning to the jury*]: Members of the jury, isn't that interesting? The police believe that Jennifer Radman murdered her brother with a stone sculpture. They believe she then drove away in her car. But they can't find any pieces of the murder weapon – not in her house, not in her garden, not in her car. [*turning back to Detective Brown*] Don't you think that's strange, Detective Brown?

WILLIAM BROWN: Perhaps.

DEFENCE: Why only perhaps?

WILLIAM BROWN [*looking at Jennifer Radman*]: Perhaps she was careful. Perhaps she cleaned the car, put the sculpture in a bag and threw it away somewhere.

DEFENCE [*angrily*]: But we don't know, do we? Now, another question. Did you look for fingerprints in Michael Boxer's house?

WILLIAM BROWN: We did. We found Mrs Radman's fingerprints, of course. But there was a meeting of the people who lived in Michael Boxer's road at his house that afternoon. There were about twenty people in his sitting room. So there were a lot of different fingerprints, and many of them weren't clear.

DEFENCE: But perhaps some of those fingerprints were the murderer's. And I don't mean Mrs Radman's.

WILLIAM BROWN [*looking bored*]: It's possible.

DEFENCE: Thank you, Detective Brown. I have no more questions. [*He sits down.*]

Scene 5

CLERK: Call Mr Simon Nichols.

[*Simon Nichols comes into the court and goes to the witness box.*]

PROSECUTION: Can you tell us how you know the defendant, Mr Nichols?

SIMON NICHOLS [*looking worried*]: Yes, I live next door to Mrs Radman.

PROSECUTION: I want you to think back to the night of December 14th.

SIMON NICHOLS: Yes, I remember that night. It was my daughter's birthday.

PROSECUTION: Where do you work?

SIMON NICHOLS: I work in a restaurant.

PROSECUTION: And what time did you get home that night?

SIMON NICHOLS: Um – at about 10.45.

PROSECUTION: Did you notice anything on the road outside the defendant's house when you returned?

SIMON NICHOLS: Um – no, I didn't notice her car.

PROSECUTION [*turning to the jury*]: Members of the jury, you remember that Michael Boxer was killed between 10 o'clock and 11.30. Mr Nichols did not see the defendant's car at 10.45 on the night of the murder. [*speaking loudly and clearly*] He says that at 10.45 she was not at home! I have no more questions. [*He sits down.*]

DEFENCE [*standing*]: Mr Nichols, can you really be sure that you didn't see Mrs Radman's car that night?

SIMON NICHOLS: I'm sure I didn't see it.

DEFENCE: Think carefully . . .

SIMON NICHOLS [*after a minute*]: Well, I can't really be sure. But I don't remember seeing it.

DEFENCE: Mr Nichols, do you like Mrs Radman?

SIMON NICHOLS: No – no, I don't. Her son plays loud music, and the smaller children are always kicking their football into my garden.

DEFENCE [*angrily*]: And so you're happy to say that you didn't see Mrs Radman's car that night.

PROSECUTION [*standing*]: Your Honour . . .

JUDGE: Mr Giles, you cannot suggest that.

DEFENCE: I'm sorry, Mr Nichols. I have no more questions. [*He sits down.*]

JUDGE: Thank you. We will start again tomorrow at 9 o'clock.

[*The judge leaves the court and people then begin to leave by a different door.*]

Act 3 Tuesday Morning

Scene 1

[*People in the court are talking excitedly. When the judge comes in, the talking stops immediately. The judge sits down.*]

JUDGE: Please sit down so we can begin.

[*Everyone sits down.*]

CLERK: Mrs Jennifer Radman, please come to the witness box.

[*Jennifer Radman goes to the witness box. She looks very pale.*]

DEFENCE [*standing*]: Do you work, Mrs Radman?

JENNIFER RADMAN [*coughing and looking very nervous*]: Only a few hours a week. I'm a single parent and I'm bringing up four children alone. When the younger two were very small, I couldn't work. I've had problems because I never had enough money. But now I'm going to find a good job and pay my debts.

DEFENCE: Thank you. Can you tell the court what happened on the night of December 14th?

JENNIFER RADMAN: Yes . . . I left the house at about 8 o'clock to visit my brother. The journey takes about twenty minutes at that time of night.

DEFENCE: Why did you go to see him?

JENNIFER RADMAN: I had debts and I needed help. I didn't want to lose my flat.

DEFENCE: And did he agree to lend you the money?

JENNIFER RADMAN: No, he didn't.

DEFENCE: I see. And what happened then?

JENNIFER RADMAN [*looking uncomfortable*]: We – we quarrelled. And we had a fight.

DEFENCE: Who started the fight, you or your brother?

JENNIFER RADMAN: Michael did. He was very rude to me that night. He called me terrible names. And then he hit me – across the face. So I scratched his face. [*She looks at the jury.*] And then I left.

DEFENCE: What time did you leave?

JENNIFER RADMAN: I'm not sure exactly, but I got back about 10.00 p.m. The 10 o'clock news was just starting. My son and his girlfriend were in the sitting room. The other children were in bed.

DEFENCE: Mrs Radman, when the police first questioned you, what did you tell them about your face?

JENNIFER RADMAN: I said, 'I walked into a door.' I was very frightened. They thought *I* was the murderer!

DEFENCE: The police found dust from the murder weapon on your clothes, Mrs Radman.

JENNIFER RADMAN: I did walk round the room while we were talking. I touched things. I probably touched the sculpture. But that doesn't mean I killed my own brother!

DEFENCE: Another question, Mrs Radman. Did you know what was in your brother's will?

JENNIFER RADMAN [*almost laughing*]: No, I never thought about it. We never talked about it. He was still a young man.

DEFENCE: Did you think that perhaps he was leaving money for you in his will?

JENNIFER RADMAN: No, I didn't. Michael never liked me, even when I was a child. He was often unkind to me. He didn't help me with money when he was alive.

DEFENCE: Mrs Radman, the prosecution believes that you came back after 10 o'clock – at 10.30 or later. What's your answer to that?

JENNIFER RADMAN: You can ask my son. He was there. Nobody asks their son to lie in court for them. I was home at about 10 o'clock.

DEFENCE: We have heard that your brother was killed with his own statue. Did you ever try to lift that statue?

JENNIFER RADMAN: No, I didn't. [*angrily*] I don't understand why I'm here. That stone sculpture was too heavy for me. Find it, and then you'll know. Look at me – I'm not a strong person. I don't understand why the police aren't looking for the real murderer. A man phoned Michael before he died. *He* wanted to kill him. The police wanted me to agree to a charge of manslaughter. But I refused – [*loudly*] because I didn't kill my brother.

DEFENCE: Thank you. I have no more questions. [*He sits down.*]

Scene 2

PROSECUTION [*standing*]: Mrs Radman, you hated your brother, didn't you?

JENNIFER RADMAN [*speaking angrily*]: No! I didn't *like* him – he was never kind to me.

PROSECUTION: You hated him. You killed him because he refused to help you.

JENNIFER RADMAN: That's not true!

PROSECUTION: Your father left Michael money. You hoped for that money after Michael's death, didn't you?

JENNIFER RADMAN [*coldly*]: No.

PROSECUTION: Michael Boxer was killed between 10 o'clock and 11.30 on December 14th. You decided to kill your brother. You decided this before you went to his house that night. You drove there. You had a fight. When your brother turned his back, you picked up the sculpture. You were strong that night because you were so angry. You hit your brother on the head and killed him. That's right, isn't it?

[*Jennifer Radman is silent for a minute.*]

JENNIFER RADMAN [*slowly*]: No. And if that's true, why didn't I take a knife or something with me?

PROSECUTION: Perhaps you did! But perhaps you were cleverer than that. You used the sculpture and threw it away later.

JENNIFER RADMAN: I did not kill my brother.

PROSECUTION: There was dust from the sculpture on your clothes, Mrs Radman. How did it get there?

JENNIFER RADMAN: I touched it when I walked round the room. I probably touched my clothes.

PROSECUTION: I don't think so. After you killed Michael, what did you do with the murder weapon, Mrs Radman? [*Jennifer Radman is silent.*] Your neighbour didn't see your car outside your house at 10.45 because you weren't back from your brother's house yet!

JENNIFER RADMAN [*speaking quietly*]: That's not true. The car wasn't there because my son was out in it. He went to get some food. You can ask him.

PROSECUTION: We will. Mrs Radman, why did you lie to the police about the bruise on your face?

JENNIFER RADMAN: I was frightened.

PROSECUTION: You were right to be frightened, Mrs Radman. You are a murderer. [*Jennifer Radman looks at him but says nothing.*] I have no more questions, your Honour. [*He sits down.*]

Scene 3

CLERK: Call Mrs Alice O'Connell.

[*Alice O'Connell comes into the court and goes to the witness box.*]

DEFENCE: Mrs O'Connell, you are the head teacher of Abbey School, isn't that right?

ALICE O'CONNELL: Yes, I am.

DEFENCE: How do you know Mrs Radman?

ALICE O'CONNELL: Mrs Radman's sixteen-year-old daughter, Helen, goes to my school.

'You are a murderer.'

DEFENCE: Can you give us your opinion of Mrs Radman?
ALICE O'CONNELL [*warmly*]: Yes. I've known Mrs Radman for five years, since her daughter started at my school. Helen's a polite and intelligent girl, and Mrs Radman's an excellent mother. She always comes to parents' evenings. She seems a kind, loving woman.
DEFENCE: Thank you, Mrs O'Connell. I have no more questions. [*He sits down.*]
PROSECUTION [*standing*]: Did you know about the defendant's money problems, Mrs O'Connell?
ALICE O'CONNELL [*coldly*]: Yes, we did discuss them once. It was difficult for her to pay for Helen's school trips.
PROSECUTION: Sometimes people seem kind, but there's another side to them. Haven't you noticed that?
ALICE O'CONNELL: I think I understand people very well. I feel sure that Jennifer Radman isn't a murderer.
PROSECUTION: I have no more questions. [*He sits down.*]

Scene 4

CLERK: Call Miss Sarah Rose.

[*Sarah Rose comes into the court and walks to the witness box. She is smiling as she comes in.*]

DEFENCE: What do you do, Miss Rose?
SARAH ROSE: I have three young children. I look after them.
DEFENCE: Do you know Mrs Radman?
SARAH ROSE: Yes. I live next door to her.
DEFENCE: What did you see on the night of December 14th?
SARAH ROSE: I was in the kitchen when a car stopped outside. I looked out and saw Jennifer. It was about 10 o'clock.
DEFENCE: Thank you. What do you think of Mrs Radman?

SARAH ROSE [*clearly*]: She's a good mother and a kind woman. She always helps me if I have a problem. She's not a violent person.

DEFENCE: Your witness, Mr Frost. [*He sits down.*]

PROSECUTION [*standing*]: Miss Rose, are you *sure* that Mrs Radman arrived back at 10 o'clock? Perhaps it was later. Please think carefully.

[*Sarah Rose is silent for a minute and looks uncomfortable.*]

SARAH ROSE: It's possible that it was a little later.

PROSECUTION: Was it perhaps 10.30, not 10 o'clock? Or later? 10.45?

SARAH ROSE [*looking nervous*]: I don't know, I can't be sure. I think it was around 10 o'clock.

PROSECUTION: Thank you. I have one more question, Miss Rose. Did the defendant wash her car the next day?

SARAH ROSE [*surprised*]: Yes – yes, she did. It was a Sunday and she cleans her car every Sunday.

PROSECUTION: Members of the jury, Mrs Radman washed her car the day after her brother's murder. Perhaps she needed to clean it. Perhaps she wanted to be sure that there was no dust from the sculpture in the car. Thank you, Miss Rose. I have no more questions. [*He sits down.*]

JUDGE: The court will stop for lunch. We will begin again at 2.30.

Act 4 Tuesday Afternoon

Scene 1

[*The jury and spectators are talking. Mr Giles is talking to Jennifer Radman. The judge comes into the court and everyone stands and stops talking. The judge sits down.*]

JUDGE: Please sit down. Let's begin.
CLERK: Call Mr Jonathan Peters.

[*Jonathan Peters comes into the courtroom and goes to the witness box.*]

DEFENCE: Did you know Michael Boxer, Mr Peters?
JONATHAN PETERS [*looking round the court*]: Yes, I knew Michael for about nine years. I met him through a friend.
DEFENCE: Did you like him?
JONATHAN PETERS: Yes. Michael was a good friend. But he could – sometimes – get very angry. Only when he had a lot to drink.
DEFENCE: Was he ever violent?
JONATHAN PETERS: Well, I remember once . . . I was with Michael and one of his girlfriends, and Michael hit her. I saw him.
DEFENCE: Michael Boxer was a policeman. Was he violent with criminals too?
JONATHAN PETERS [*looking worried*]: Yes, I think so. Only dangerous criminals, of course. There were people who hated him.
DEFENCE: How do you know that, Mr Peters?
JONATHAN PETERS: In the months before he died, Michael was worried about two men who were out of prison. He told me. He said, 'I think they'll come after me.'
DEFENCE: 'Come after me'? What do you think he meant by that?
JONATHAN PETERS: He meant 'hurt him'.
DEFENCE: Were there any letters or phone calls from these men?

JONATHAN PETERS: I know about two phone calls. Each time a man said, 'We're going to get you, Michael Boxer.' Then the man put the phone down. Michael told me about them.

DEFENCE: Was he frightened?

JONATHAN PETERS: Yes, he was. He changed the locks on his house a week before he died.

DEFENCE: Thank you. I have no more questions. [*He sits down.*]

PROSECUTION [*standing*]: Mr Peters, did Michael Boxer ever really hurt anyone?

JONATHAN PETERS: You mean, so they had to go to hospital? I don't know. I don't think so.

PROSECUTION: Another question . . . Did Michael Boxer ever discuss his sister with you?

JONATHAN PETERS: Yes, he did. He didn't like her. She always wanted money from him.

PROSECUTION: Michael Boxer didn't leave his sister any money when he died. Did he tell you about his plans for his money?

JONATHAN PETERS: No, of course not. He was secretive about money and it wasn't my business.

PROSECUTION: Right. Now, the phone calls that you've talked about. Mr Boxer didn't report them to the police – they know nothing about them. Why not?

JONATHAN PETERS: I don't know. I wanted him to report them.

PROSECUTION: Thank you. I have no more questions. [*He sits down.*]

Scene 2

CLERK: Call Mr Daniel Radman.

[*Daniel Radman comes into the court and goes to the witness box. He looks nervous.*]

DEFENCE: Mr Radman, are you Jennifer Radman's son?

DANIEL RADMAN: Yes, I'm her oldest child.

DEFENCE: How old are you, Mr Radman?

DANIEL RADMAN: Eighteen.

DEFENCE: What do you do?

DANIEL RADMAN: I work for a builder.

DEFENCE: And where do you live, Mr Radman?

DANIEL RADMAN: With my mum.

DEFENCE: Do you give her money for food and rent?

DANIEL RADMAN: Yes.

DEFENCE: You've had some trouble with the law, haven't you?

DANIEL RADMAN [*looking uncomfortable*]: Yes.

DEFENCE: Can you tell the court what happened?

DANIEL RADMAN [*after a minute or two*]: I was at a football game and I had a fight. I went to court – but not to prison. It was nothing.

DEFENCE: Did you hurt the person you had this fight with?

DANIEL RADMAN: Yes. I – I broke his leg.

DEFENCE: You broke his leg . . . Now, can you tell the court what happened on the night of December 14th?

DANIEL RADMAN: We watched TV. My mum came home about 10 o'clock with a big bruise on her face. She told me what happened. Me and Sharon, my girlfriend, were really upset. Then Mum went to bed. I went out in the car to get a Chinese meal. I came back and Sharon and I ate it. Then we went to bed. That's it.

DEFENCE: What time did you go out?

DANIEL RADMAN: About 10.40.

DEFENCE: Thank you. [*He turns to the jury.*] Members of the jury, Mrs Radman's neighbour, Simon Nichols, isn't sure that he saw the Radmans' car at 10.45. But Daniel Radman, not his mother, was out in the car at that time. [*turning to Mr Frost*] Your witness, Mr Frost. [*He sits down.*]

'My mum came home with a big bruise on her face.'

PROSECUTION: Your girlfriend, Sharon Phillips, is going to have your child, isn't she, Mr Radman? Are you going to marry her?

DANIEL RADMAN: Er . . . Yes, I am.

PROSECUTION: Where did you go for your Chinese meal, Mr Radman?

DANIEL RADMAN: To Peking House in the High Street.

PROSECUTION: Really? I have a statement here from the manager of the Peking House. Mrs Colly, will you please pass these copies around. [*The clerk takes them to the judge, the jury and Daniel Radman.*] The manager says that he doesn't remember seeing you. He also says that you usually go there on a Friday night, not on a Saturday. Is that correct?

DANIEL RADMAN: Oh . . . Well, yes, usually. But sometimes I go on a Saturday.

PROSECUTION: It's not true that you got a Chinese meal on that Saturday, Mr Radman. You're lying about your mother. You're trying to protect her, aren't you?

DANIEL RADMAN [*looking very upset*]: No! I'm not lying. She *did* come back about 10 o'clock. And I *did* go out for some food.

PROSECUTION: Mr Radman, your uncle wasn't married and he didn't have any children. So after your grandfather's death, your mother was his closest relative, wasn't she?

DANIEL RADMAN: Yes.

PROSECUTION: Don't people usually leave money to their close relatives when they die?

DANIEL RADMAN: Probably. But not in our family. My uncle didn't like my mum. He didn't leave us anything.

PROSECUTION: But she didn't know that until after his death, did she?

DANIEL RADMAN: She didn't *know*, but she could guess!

PROSECUTION: Your Honour, I have no more questions. [*He sits down.*]

Scene 3

CLERK: Call Sharon Phillips.

[*Sharon Phillips comes into the court and goes to the witness box.*]

DEFENCE [*standing and speaking kindly*]: Do you live with the Radman family, Miss Phillips?

SHARON PHILLIPS [*speaking quickly*]: No, but I often stay the night there.

DEFENCE: Can you tell the court what happened on the night of December 14th?

SHARON PHILLIPS: Jennifer – Dan's mum – came home about 10 o'clock. There was a big bruise on her face. She told us what happened. Then she went to bed. Dan went out and got a Chinese meal. We stayed up and watched TV. We went to bed about midnight.

DEFENCE: Thank you. Your witness, Mr Frost. [*He sits down.*]

PROSECUTION: When are you going to have your baby, Miss Phillips?

SHARON PHILLIPS: In six months.

PROSECUTION: And will you marry Daniel Radman?

SHARON PHILLIPS: Yes.

PROSECUTION: Do you love him?

SHARON PHILLIPS [*red-faced*]: Yes, I do.

PROSECUTION: So you want to protect Daniel's mother, don't you, Miss Phillips?

SHARON PHILLIPS [*quietly and slowly*]: No, it's true – Jennifer didn't go out again.

PROSECUTION: You don't seem very sure of that, Miss Phillips.

SHARON PHILLIPS: She didn't!

PROSECUTION: I have no more questions.

Scene 4

JUDGE: Mr Frost, will you speak to the jury for the last time, please?

PROSECUTION: Yes, your Honour. [*standing and turning to the jury*] Members of the jury, remember Jennifer Radman's words to her brother at her father's funeral: 'You should be dead too.' These are not the words of a kind, loving sister. We know that Michael Boxer opened the door to his killer. If the killer had a weapon, why didn't he kill Mr Boxer with it? No, Mr Boxer knew his murderer well. Mrs Radman killed her brother. She killed him because she wanted his money. Her son lied for her because he loves her. Sharon Phillips lied too. When the police first questioned Mrs Radman, *she* lied to them. Remember that. She is a murderer. [*He sits down.*]

JUDGE: Mr Giles?

DEFENCE [*standing*]: Members of the jury, the prosecution has not proved that Mrs Radman killed her brother. Remember that Mrs Stanton never lifted the sculpture. It was too heavy. How could a small woman hit someone on the head with it? It's not possible. We know that other people hated Michael Boxer — the two men who were out of prison, for example. Michael Boxer probably opened his door to someone with a weapon. They followed him to the sitting room. There, they picked up the sculpture and killed him with it. The police have the wrong person. Jennifer Radman did not kill her brother. [*He sits down.*]

JUDGE: Did Mrs Radman kill her brother? There is no easy answer to this question, members of the jury. There are a number of things that you must think about. Did Jennifer Radman return home at 10 o'clock, as her son and his girlfriend say? Or are they protecting her? Did the defendant perhaps hit her brother with the sculpture without meaning to kill him? You must think about all the facts, members of the jury. Then you must decide what happened. You must be *sure* that Mrs Radman murdered her brother. If you are not sure, then she must go free.

[*The judge gets up and leaves the court. Members of the jury leave by a different door. Mr Giles talks for a minute or two to Jennifer Radman. Then two policemen take Jennifer Radman out of the courtroom. Everyone leaves.*]

ACTIVITIES

Act 1

Before you read

1 In this play, the police believe that a woman has murdered her brother. List some possible reasons for the murder of a brother or sister.
2 What are these sentences in your language? Find the words in *italics* in your dictionary. They are all used in the play.
   a She gets married in the third *scene* of the second *act*.
   b I visited my bank *manager* because I was in *debt*. I couldn't pay my *rent*.
   c We read our father's *will* after the *funeral*, when we were still very *upset*.
   d The *quarrel* became *violent*, and after the other man's death Paul was *charged* with murder.

After you read

3 Answer these questions.
   a How exactly was Michael Boxer killed?
   b Why do the police think that Jennifer Radman killed her brother?
4 Imagine that you are one of these witnesses. Tell a friend why you went to court. Explain how you feel about Jennifer Radman.
   Gina Lopez   Peter Lampton   Tim Radley   Robert Woods
   Matthew Foley

Act 2

Before you read

5 Why did Jennifer visit her brother on the night of 14 December, do you think? What happened that evening?
6 Write sentences using these words. Check their meaning in your dictionary.
   a *bruise*, *weapon*
   b *dust*, *sculpture*
   c *fingernail*, *scratch*
   d *fingerprint*, *forensic officer*

After you read

7 Complete the sentences.
  a Michael Boxer was hit on the head with a stone . . . . . .
  b Mrs Stanton never . . . . . the sculpture.
  c Jennifer is . . . . . and . . . . . than Mrs Stanton.
  d There were long . . . . . on Michael Boxer's face.
  e The police found stone . . . . . on Jennifer's clothes.
  f The doors and windows were all . . . . . .
  g The police could not find the murder . . . . . .

8 Explain the importance of these times:
10.00–11.30 p.m.   9.30 p.m.   10.45 p.m.   11.00 a.m.

9 Work in pairs with another student. Act out this discussion between the two lawyers.
  Student A: You are the prosecution lawyer. Explain why you think Jennifer killed her brother.
  Student B: You are the defence lawyer. Explain why you disagree.

Acts 3 and 4

Before you read

10 What do you think Jennifer Radman's defence will be?
11 Find the word *manslaughter* in your dictionary. What is the difference between manslaughter and murder? Which is more serious? Give an example of each crime.

After you read

12 How does each of these witnesses help Jennifer's defence? Do you think any of them are lying?
Alice O'Connell   Sarah Rose   Jonathan Peters   Daniel Radman   Sharon Phillips
13 Work in small groups. Imagine that you are members of the jury. You must decide if Jennifer killed her brother.

Writing

14 Imagine that you work for a newspaper. Write a short report about what happened in court.
15 Write the story of what Jennifer did on the evening of 14 December.

16 What does the jury decide, in your opinion? What are their reasons?

17 The jury decide that Jennifer did not kill her brother. Write what happens next. Write about fifteen lines.

> **THE WRITER'S OPINION**
> Jennifer Radman did not kill her brother – but she is protecting her son. Daniel is a strong young man who works for a builder. We know that he can be violent. When his mother returned home with a bruise on her face, he was upset and angry. He drove to his uncle's house and Michael Boxer took him into the sitting room. When Michael turned his back for a minute, Daniel hit him with the sculpture. Daniel took the sculpture home and told his mother and his girlfriend everything. Jennifer told him to drive somewhere and throw the sculpture away. The next day, she cleaned the car.

Answers for the Activities in this book are available from your local Pearson Education office. Alternatively, write to: Penguin Readers, Marketing Department, Pearson Education, Edinburgh Gate, Harlow, Essex, CM20 2JE.
Also visit www.penguinreaders.com for your free Factsheet for this book.